QUIT
SMOKING
TODAY

Without Gaining Weight

www.booksattransworld.co.uk

QUIT SMOKING TODAY

Without Gaining Weight

PAUL McKENNA PhD

Edited by Michael Neill

BANTAM PRESS

LONDON · TORONTO · SYDNEY · AUCKLAND · JOHANNESBURG

TRANSWORLD PUBLISHERS
61–63 Uxbridge Road, London W5 5SA
a division of the Random House Group Ltd
www.booksattransworld.co.uk

First published in Great Britain
in 2007 by Bantam Press
a division of Transworld Publishers

A CIP catalogue record for this book
is available from the British Library.

ISBN 9780593055366

Illustrations copyright © Gillian Blease 2007

Addresses for Random House Group Ltd companies outside the UK
can be found at: www.randomhouse.co.uk
The Random House Group Ltd Reg. No. 954009

The Random House Group Ltd makes every effort to ensure that the papers used in its
books are made from trees that have been legally sourced from well-managed and credibly
certified forests. Our paper procurement policy can be found at:
www.randomhouse.co.uk/paper.htm

Printed and bound in Great Britain by Clays Ltd, St Ives plc
Design by Fiona Andreanelli

6 8 10 9 7

Mixed Sources
Product group from well-managed
forests and other controlled sources
www.fsc.org Cert no. TT-COC-2139
© 1996 Forest Stewardship Council
FSC

For Uncle John

I would like to thank Dr Richard Bandler, Dr Roger Callaghan, Dr Natheera Indrasenan, Dr Ronald Ruden, Dr Hugh Willbourn, Dr Farhad Neave, Trudy Edmonson, Mike Osborne and Robert Kirby. Thanks to Larry Finlay, Doug Young and Mari Roberts for continued support and suggesting I write this book. Thank you to all the clients over the years who have helped me develop this system.

Lastly thanks to Michael Neill whose immense support and contribution to my work continues.

CONTENTS

A QUICK NOTE
FROM PAUL

There are two kinds of smokers – those who know they want to quit but don't think they can, and those who think they can quit any time they want but are too scared to find out if they really can.

In both cases, the real question is: who's in charge – you or the cigarettes?

If you're in the category of people who say, 'I could quit any time I want – I just don't want to,' I want you to know that that isn't you talking – it's the cigarettes.

You'd probably like to think you're in control and that smoking is up to you – but if you have ever tried to quit before and failed, you also probably know that's not really true. As the famous French writer Charles Baudelaire wrote, 'The greatest trick the devil ever pulled off was convincing the world he didn't exist.'

Here's how you can find out for sure. If you're someone who wants to quit but doesn't think they can, go through each exercise in the book with an open mind. You'll quickly find the whole process to be far easier than you imagined.

If, on the other hand, you're someone who thinks they can quit but doesn't want to, go through the system anyway. You'll soon find out how much power you really have or how much of your life you've given away to cigarettes, and how much this book can help you.

You can always go back to smoking when you're done if you really want – but chances are that once you taste freedom, you'll never go back to the taste of cigarettes again.

To your success,

Paul McKenna

QUIT
SMOKING
TODAY

SESSION ONE

•

Getting Started

Getting Started

Congratulations – you are about to quit smoking forever!

It doesn't matter if you have smoked all your life, if you have tried to quit many times before and failed or if you don't believe this system will work for you. All you have to do is follow my instructions fully and completely and you will never smoke again. Not only that, you will do so with a sense of near effortlessness and you will be highly unlikely to gain any weight.

When I was discussing with my publisher why my quit-smoking system was different to others, I mentioned that people are highly unlikely to put on weight because it treats the core reason why people smoke, not just the symptom. In fact, a recent study revealed that only 3 per cent of the people using my system to quit smoking gained any weight at all, and over 6 per cent actually lost weight while quitting smoking.

I have spent the last twenty years studying human behaviour and developing this revolutionary approach to quitting smoking without gaining weight. I know exactly why you smoke and how to stop it for good. Your mind is like a computer, and like a computer it has its own software. Each one of your habits, healthy or deadly, is operating right now in your mind like the programmes on a computer.

Over the course of this book, we are going to reprogramme your mind through the various imagination exercises and with the hypnosis CD that accompanies it. By the time you finish this book and have listened to the CD every day for at least two weeks, a cigarette will never seem the same to you again.

There are, however, a couple of things you need to know before we begin.

1. I do not believe that smoking or cigarettes are 'evil'

If you want to smoke, smoke – I do not have a moral issue with it. I believe what you do with your body is your business. In fact, if you want to eat mud I believe that should be up to you – not your friends, not your family and not the government.

Smoking is nothing more than an external means to change the way you feel, a practice that is widely accepted in our culture. Food, alcohol, drugs, sex, gambling, television and shopping all change the way we feel as well. The reason some of these things are seen as problems and others are not is that in the long-term, there are massive negative health consequences to prolonged exposure to nicotine.

As a drug of choice, smoking is not a smart one if you weigh up the temporary good feelings a cigarette gives you against the likelihood of an early and in most cases slow and painful death. Let's face it – if I asked you to swallow a cyanide pill or inhale asbestos dust each day in exchange for some temporary feelings of relaxation, would you do it? Probably not. But I'll bet you're dying for a cigarette, even as you read these words.

My uncle John was a heavy smoker. He had just retired and was ready to enjoy the easy life. Out of the blue, he had a stroke. He could hardly speak and was confined to a wheelchair. But the urge to smoke doesn't go away even when your life is clearly on the line.

It is this total lack of freedom that cigarettes cause that I find so difficult to take. As long as you feel like you have to smoke, you are a slave to your cigarettes. You work for them. The moment you can consciously choose whether to smoke or to quit, you are back in control and you are free.

My goal in this book isn't just to help you to quit smoking – it is to help you take your life back. No less, no more.

2. I can't make you quit smoking – sorry!

A man came up to me at a party some years ago and said, 'You're that hypnotist off the telly, aren't you?' I said that I was and attempted to make a gracious exit, as I knew what was coming.

He said, 'I'll tell you what – I'll give you £100,000 if you make me stop smoking right now.' I tried several times to put him off politely but eventually I told him, 'I think it's time you took some personal responsibility for your life.'

In one recent study, 90 per cent of smokers surveyed said they wanted to quit. So why haven't they?

It's because smoking is not a logical, rational, conscious act – it's a learned habitual response to stress and nicotine. You can't undo it with reasons or statistics – you need to actually reprogramme your mind.

Now here's the good news – I can't *make* you quit smoking, but I will *make* it significantly easier for **you** to quit by teaching you specific ways to undo your old programming and build new habits of feeling good. I will show you how to stop cravings almost before they start; to take away the feeling that you *need* cigarettes; to find all the pleasure and relaxation and more that you used to get from cigarettes in other ways.

Better still, you will be able to do all this without gaining weight.

Is it really possible to quit smoking in just one day?

Helping people to quit smoking over the years has been an interesting process. Many of them come to me hiding their resentment that someone or something has control over them.

Worse still, they think that by stopping, they are going to miss out – that they are never going to be able to have fun like they used to, or that life will become boring without cigarettes. If this is you, you are in for a wonderful surprise.

What I am about to share with you has taken me over fifteen years to develop and has been tested on over 250,000 people around the world. Unlike many other systems, it doesn't just consist of one idea or one technique. But while different techniques work for different people, the end result is the same – the decision to quit smoking and the ability to carry out that decision for life.

Together, we are going to reprogramme your mind so that smoking doesn't matter to you any more – you don't need a cigarette in order to feel good. In fact, you will feel so much healthier, happier and more alive without cigarettes that the whole idea of smoking will seem like an odd sort of memory – like something you used to do that no longer makes any sense at all.

How to use this system

I am convinced that one of the reasons my system is so successful is that the process is easy. You learn to take yourself step by step across the threshold from someone who thinks of him or herself as a 'life-long smoker' to someone who used to smoke. By the time you are finished with the exercises in this book, smoking will never seem the same to you again.

Even for those people who continue to get the occasional craving, I will be giving you specific tools you can use on the spot and in the moment to eliminate the craving and create feelings of relaxation and ease in a matter of moments.

Which brings up an interesting point ...

From time to time people say a curious thing to me: that they tried to quit smoking but 'it didn't work'. When I ask them if they really didn't quit for even a few hours, they usually admit that they did stop for a while, but after a few days, months or even in some cases years, they began smoking again.

I am always a bit dumbfounded when I hear this. If you have stopped for a day, you can stop for two days; if you stopped for two days, you can stop for two weeks; if you stopped for two weeks, you can stop for two months, two years, twenty years or even forever. If you have gone back to smoking in the past, it's for one of two reasons:

- The approach you were using wasn't the best one for you at the time.

- You stopped doing what was working.

This is why I am going to take you through so many different techniques within my system. No matter who you are, there are enough different things on offer here that you will find what works for you. All you need to do is read the book through once, including the 'frequently asked questions' section at the end of each session. These sections include information that will be helpful to you and may answer questions and eliminate doubts you didn't even know you had.

Take the time to do each exercise in turn. While any one of the exercises may be enough, the cumulative effect is more than enough to recondition *anyone's* mind and body to stop smoking and create a new, healthy you for the rest of your life.

About the CD

I have received thousands of letters and testimonials over the years from people who have quit smoking forever simply by listening to my hypnotic CDs. When you combine the hypnotic trance on the CD with the ideas and the mind-programming exercises in each session in the book, your efforts will be rewarded and success will be yours!

Whether you quit smoking after your very first session or you wait until you complete the entire system, *it is essential that you keep using the CD every day for at least two weeks*. Even though you may achieve instant success, each time you listen will reinforce the changes at the unconscious level, making the transition from smoking to health easier and more enjoyable.

Years ago, I went into a studio to record my very first hypnosis cassette (as they were in those days). The process of recording and editing the tapes took just under a week. One night towards the end of the session the studio engineer took me aside and told me he was very concerned about something. When I asked him what it was, he said that he was a forty-a-day smoker but he hadn't had a single cigarette in the past five days.

I asked him why that was a problem and he said, 'I really enjoyed smoking – I didn't want to quit.'

'So start again,' I said.

'But I don't have any desire for it any more – do you think it might be something to do with all this "quit smoking" stuff we're doing?'

He never smoked again, and over the years I have collected many stories from people who gave up even without having planned to, just by listening. There was the lady who smoked a hundred cigarettes a day and only came along to a session to keep her friend company. They both ended up relaxing during the hypnosis and quitting that day.

The point is, smoking is a habit, and all our habits are regulated by the unconscious mind. Through hypnosis, I am able to communicate directly with your unconscious. That is why it is so important that you listen to the CD with this book every day for at least two weeks, whether you believe it's helping you or not. It is!

FREQUENTLY ASKED QUESTIONS ABOUT 'GETTING STARTED'

Q. I don't have any willpower – can I still use your system?

Absolutely – because unlike other systems, this one is not based on willpower, it's based on reprogramming your mind. Besides, all smokers have willpower or they could never have got themselves addicted in the first place. You had to force your body to smoke when every cell was screaming for you to stop – now we're simply undoing the process.

It is *impossible* to stay smoking if you do all the exercises in this book and listen to the CD for at least two weeks. In fact, in following up with those few people who did not quit smoking after using this system, I found they had one thing in common – they didn't follow my instructions.

When I asked them why they would take the trouble to read the book without actually applying the system, I was amazed at the excuses they made up. Only one person was really honest with me and admitted the truth – they were terrified the system would work!

The reason people get scared of the techniques working is they think they will have to give up smoking but keep the bad feelings – in fact, the opposite is true. If you simply do each technique in turn, repeating the ones that seem particularly powerful and reinforcing the changes with the

CD, you will have control over the bad feelings and your life will change for the better.

Q. I'm worried about getting my hopes up only to be disappointed again when I don't quit or I gain weight. Will this REALLY work?

Nobody likes to feel disappointed, but how disappointed will you be if you get to the end of your life and you haven't given this system a proper testing?

Face it – if you do what you've always done, you'll get what you've always gotten. If, on the other hand, you do each exercise and listen to the CD each day for two weeks, you will have quit smoking and begun to move on with your life. The choice, as always, is yours.

Q. Surely your system only treats the habit, not the addiction. Should I use nicotine patches or gum at the same time as going through your system?

Nicotine patches, gum and sprays all deliver decreasing doses of nicotine, the addictive chemical in cigarettes, over a period of weeks. This can lead to some nasty side effects ranging from nausea to sleep disturbance. They also extend the period of time it takes you to quit.

In the end, there is only one way to quit smoking and it's this:

Decide you are never, ever going to smoke again!

That's why one of the keys to your success with this system is your level of commitment and determination to quitting smoking once and for all.

If you are ready to quit today, read on. When you are at the point where even if every technique in this book and on the CD failed you would still just go ahead and quit anyway, you are ready to get started now …

SESSION TWO

•

Why You Used
to Smoke

Why You Used to Smoke

Unless you are smoking a cigarette as you read this, it is entirely possible that you are no longer a smoker. Is that a strange concept to consider? Does it feel unusual, even foreign? This is not because it's not yet true, but rather because you are not yet in the habit of thinking about it in this way.

Do this simple exercise:

1 Add up all the time you actually spend smoking in a day. For example, if you smoke 20 a day and each cigarette lasts for about 5 minutes, you smoke for about 100 minutes (1 hour and 40 minutes) each day.

2 Subtract your answer from the 24 hours in a day. In our example above that would leave you with 22 hours and 20 minutes.

If you already spend over 22 hours a day not smoking, does it feel a bit easier to believe you could not smoke for 23 hours a day? For 23 and a half? For 23 hours and 50 minutes? Could you not smoke for 23 hours and 55 minutes?

Before you finish reading this chapter, we will do the first in a series of reprogramming exercises that will make it feel easy and natural to think of yourself as a health-conscious person who no longer smokes. Through simple imagination, repetition and reinforcement, what currently feels unusual will begin to feel more and more natural. In fact, from now on I would like you to think of yourself not as 'a smoker', but simply as one of the millions of people in the world who used to smoke but no longer choose to do so.

Now, if you think back to the last few times you smoked, you may recall that you quite enjoyed it. In fact, some smokers will tell you they love smoking, and are therefore reluctant to quit. But the good feeling they currently associate with cigarettes is actually brought about by a chemical release of endorphins (happy chemicals) into your bloodstream – and that 'happy release' is available to you in any moment, something I'm going to show you how to do a bit later in this session.

What's your story?

Every smoker has a story about why they smoke and why they don't need or even want to quit.

Here are some of the most common ones:

- Everybody has to die of something – at least I'll die from something I enjoy doing.

- If it was as bad as everyone says, it would surely be illegal.

- All the doctors who tell you to quit smoke like bloody chimneys – anyway, I reckon I get fewer colds than non-smokers.

- My boyfriend/girlfriend/friends wouldn't like me if I didn't smoke.

- If I quit, I'd be so stressed I wouldn't be any fun to be around. I owe it to my family to keep smoking.

- Given the things I have to put up with, I deserve a few cigarettes at the end of the day.

- Of course I want to give up, but I just want to finish this packet.

Whether your story is one of these or you have a unique one all your own, it's important to recognize that it's not real – it's just a story. And who would you be without that story?

Stop for a moment and imagine waking up tomorrow morning and a miracle has happened – you no longer smoke and you feel no urge or cravings. Would you still tell yourself that story about why you should keep doing it? What if you went through each day feeling great without any desire for a cigarette?

The real reason you haven't quit yet is not because of your story, it's because it is not yet up to you.

What has kept you smoking in the past is your own brain chemistry and psychological habit – the stories you tell yourself were just how you justified it to yourself afterwards.

The science of smoking

When a smoker smokes a cigarette, the crude chemicals they inhale signal their brain to release endorphins, the body's natural opiates. So it's not actually the cigarette that makes them feel good, but their body's own internal response to that cigarette.

If you've ever coughed or hacked up phlegm while smoking, even if it was only in the early days, you already know that nicotine is a poison. The difficulty nearly every person had learning to inhale (along with nausea, light-headedness and in some extreme cases vomiting) was an attempt by your body to prevent any more of the poison getting into your system.

However, the stress on your body brought on by the presence of nicotine also triggered a release of endorphins and endomorphines in order to ease the pain caused in fighting off the poison in the cigarette.

To ensure it has enough 'natural painkillers' available for any future 'attack' (i.e. cigarette), the body shuts down its natural cycle of endorphin releases, saving them up instead to combat the next infusion of poisonous chemicals.

When the anticipated endorphin release doesn't come, the smoker experiences stress and craves the endorphin release they now associate with smoking another cigarette. But this craving was created by endorphin depletion caused by the previous cigarettes!

Some smokers find this difficult to believe, but much of the stress relieved by a cigarette was actually *caused* by smoking the one before. It's a bit like being in a chemical S&M club – beating yourself up in order to feel better when you stop.

Bit by bit, smoking shuts down your body's natural system for dealing with the real stresses of life, replacing it with an artificial and ultimately deadly substitute.

As you read the next few pages and do the exercises that follow, I will be teaching you how to take back your power to experience relief from stress without cigarettes and experience even more natural pleasure. You will learn to be in charge of your internal responses instead of their victim and slave. Mastering this ability allows you to have the best of both worlds – all the good feelings you used to associate with cigarettes and the long-term health and wellbeing rewards of a healthy, smoke-free lifestyle.

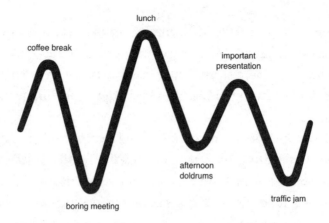

Cigarettes and stress

Every day has its emotional ups and downs. Something happens and you get excited. Then there's a lull and you get a bit bored. Then there's something else to be done and you've got to somehow find the energy to do it. And when in doubt, people tend to do what has worked in the past. They reach for another cigarette in an attempt to make them feel more relaxed and in control when they are stressed and to lift them up and refresh them when they are bored.

But take a look at this chart to see what's really going on:

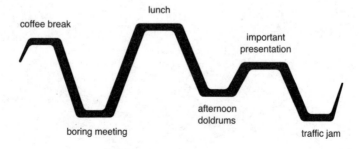

By smoking, you have been cutting off the peaks and picking up the troughs of your emotional experience all day long, reducing your stress and lifting your mood any time you began to feel bored. So if you just stopped smoking without using any of the mind-reprogramming techniques in this book, you would suddenly feel more peaks and troughs – in other words, you will be feeling more of your feelings, both high and low.

If you just stopped smoking without using any of the techniques in this system, the endorphins in your body would not immediately know that another 'cigarette attack' was not coming. They would continue to accumulate, waiting for the next cigarette to trigger their release into your bloodstream so they could do their job and make you feel better.

The cycle works like this:

Feel stress – Smoke cigarette – Signal endorphin release –
Feel temporary relaxation – Exhaust endorphin production –
Feel increased stress

Let me make one thing clear – stress is not bad in and of itself. Mild stress helps to energize your body and motivates you to take action. So while you will never eliminate all the stress in your life, by even slightly increasing your stress tolerance and lowering your stress levels, the entire mechanism will reset and you will find yourself back in control. This is what I will show you how to do in the very next session.

Creating 'instant calm'

I remember working with a woman who had smoked for thirty years and had tried to quit several times, using everything from willpower to patches to traditional hypnotherapy to imagining her kids screaming and crying their eyes out because she was going to die and leave them all alone.

Each time she started to quit, she began to put on weight. She would begin smoking again to lose the weight, and the cycle would continue.

Nothing worked until I taught her this simple exercise you are about to learn. In just a few moments, you will be able to alter the baseline settings of your stress levels in your brain and in your body. Once you take control of your own stress levels, you will naturally feel more relaxed in many situations in your life. You will no longer be dependent on the crutch of cigarettes to help you.

This is true no matter how bad it may seem to you now. When we have finished reprogramming your mind, you will have significantly more control over your desire and you will be naturally drawn to make healthier choices about what you do and don't put into your body. This is because the effects of any drug you take are not caused by the drug but by your body's response to it. The release of neuro-chemicals in your body in response to the presence of the chemicals in the drug is what causes the feelings.

In one extraordinary experiment in America, heroin addicts were hypnotized and given the suggestion that they had just taken a dose of heroin. All of them experienced the endorphin release associated with the drug without any outside chemicals actually entering their body. Through repeated use of this process, they were able to easily come off the heroin without experiencing the normal withdrawal symptoms.

In this next exercise, we are going to use the same basic technique to create good feelings inside your body – the same good feelings you used to associate with smoking cigarettes. By repeatedly doing this exercise and reinforcing it with the hypnotic suggestions on the CD, you will be able to ease yourself off any physical addiction you may have to nicotine without the worry, stress or struggle most people experience ...

THE CALM ANCHOR

Before you do this technique for yourself, read through each step so that you know exactly what to do.

1 Remember a time when you felt really, really calm – at peace and in control. Fully return to it now, seeing what you saw, hearing what you heard and feeling how good you felt. (If you can't remember a time, imagine how wonderful it would feel to be totally at peace – if you had all the ease, comfort and self-control you could ever need!)

2 As you keep running through this experience in your mind, make the colours brighter and richer, the sounds crisper and the feelings stronger. When you are feeling these good feelings, squeeze the thumb and middle finger of your **right hand** together. You are associating this particular pressure in this particular place with this particular emotion. Run through this memory several times until you feel a lovely sense of inner peace and calm.

3 Now go through this relaxing memory at least five more times while continuing to squeeze your thumb and middle finger together to really lock in these good feelings. You will know you have done it enough when all you need to do is squeeze your fingers together and you can easily

remember the feelings of calm and relaxation spreading through your body.

4 Next, think about a situation that in the past you would have found mildly stressful. (We will deal with any 'high stress' situations in the next exercise.) Once again, squeeze your thumb and middle finger together. Feel that calm feeling spreading through your body and imagine taking it with you into that stressful situation. Imagine everything going perfectly, exactly the way that you want. See what you'll see, hear what you'll hear and feel how good it feels to be so much calmer and in control in this situation.

5 Now, still squeezing your thumb and finger together, remember that calm feeling of being in control and once again imagine being in that situation that used to seem stressful. This time, imagine a few challenges occurring and notice yourself handling all the challenges perfectly. See what you'll see, hear what you'll hear and feel how good it feels to be so much calmer and in control in this situation.

6 Stop and think about that situation now. Notice the difference from only a few minutes ago. Do you feel less stressed and more in control? If not, just repeat the exercise until you do!

Each time you do this exercise, it will become easier and easier to experience feelings of relaxation and calm 'at your fingertips' …

When you feel comfortable with this exercise, you are ready to reprogramme yourself to be generally more relaxed – to experience a greater sense of ease and wellbeing in any area of your life.

The human mind generalizes as a learning principle. These generalizations are like computer programmes that allow you to do things on autopilot. For example, as a child you learn how to open a door. After you have done this several times, you generalize about all doors everywhere. Otherwise, you would have to literally learn how to go in and out of a room every single time.

Before starting on this system, you held a generalization about stress in your unconscious mind that told you smoking was the easiest way to control your feelings. You would either have a cigarette whenever you felt stressed or reward yourself with one when the stressful incident was over.

Now, we are going to change that generalization for good. We are going to reprogramme your body's relaxation response so that it happens automatically whenever it's needed, without a cigarette, without food, almost without thinking. You will feel calmer and more in control in every area of your life.

Your nervous system cannot tell the difference between a real and vividly imagined experience. So each time you imagine a stressful situation, you will experience that stress almost as much as if it were really happening now. By imagining those same situations but this time responding with inner calm instead of stress, you are reprogramming yourself to feel better in the real world. When you feel better, you will be able to handle all those situations differently in the future.

TAKE CONTROL OF YOUR LIFE

Before you do this technique for yourself, read through each step so that you know exactly what to do.

1 What I want you to do is to pick the five most significant stresses currently active in your life. These aren't necessarily to do with smoking, but if they are it's all right. Write them down to make it easier to remember as you go through the following.

   Once you've created your list, we are going to systematically lower the stress levels on each one of them. This will create a new generalization in your unconscious mind, leading to a lower overall stress level in your life.

2 Choose one of the five situations to begin the process of change. Now, using the calm anchor you created in the previous exercise, think about this situation you normally find stressful and squeeze your thumb and finger together.

   Feel that calm feeling spreading through your body and imagine taking it with you into that stressful situation. Imagine everything going perfectly, exactly the way you want. See what you'll see, hear what you'll hear and feel how good it feels to be so much calmer and in control in this situation.

3 Now, still squeezing your thumb and finger together, remember that calm feeling of being in control, and once again imagine being in that situation that used to seem stressful. This time, imagine a few challenges occurring and notice yourself handling all the challenges perfectly. See what you'll see, hear what you'll hear and feel how good it feels to be so much calmer and in control in this situation.

4 Stop and think about that situation now. Notice the difference from only a few minutes ago. Do you feel less stressed and more in control? If not, just repeat the exercise until you do!

5 Repeat this process with each one of the five situations until you feel significantly more relaxed and in control. The process of generalization has now begun!

FREQUENTLY ASKED QUESTIONS ABOUT 'WHY YOU USED TO SMOKE'

Q. I've smoked for over half my life, and am worried I've done irreparable damage to my body. At this point, is it even worth quitting?

Absolutely! While sooner is obviously better, it's never too late to quit. And the health benefits begin almost immediately.

You may have already seen these interesting facts taken from the US Surgeon General's report on the benefits of quitting for life:

After 20 minutes Your blood pressure drops to a level close to that before the last cigarette. The temperature of your hands and feet increases to normal.

After 8 hours The carbon-monoxide level in your blood drops to normal.

After 24 hours Your chance of a heart attack decreases.

Within 3 months Your circulation improves and your lung function increases up to 30 per cent.

After 1 year The excess risk of coronary heart disease is half that of a smoker's.

After 5 years Stroke risk is reduced to that of someone who has never smoked.

After 10 years The lung-cancer death rate is about half that of a continuing smoker's. The risk of cancer of the mouth, throat, oesophagus, bladder, kidney and pancreas decreases.

After 15 years The risk of coronary heart disease is that of someone who has never smoked.

Q. I've heard people say that it's as hard to give up cigarettes as it is to give up heroin. Is that true?

Having assisted a number of people in going beyond their heroin addiction, I can assure you that it is not true. Unless within hours of not having a cigarette you are sitting in a pile of your own vomit shaking uncontrollably, chances are it will be easier for you to give up cigarettes than you think.

Q. How can you say this is going to be easy? I'm trying to change the habit of a lifetime!

If you didn't use the kinds of techniques in this system, you might find it difficult, but the reality is that you can change any habit in a matter of moments. For example, I travel back and forth between the United Kingdom and United States on a regular basis. Although I have been driving on the left side of the road for my entire life, within minutes I am able to make the adjustment to the right side and proceed safely.

As a therapist, I help people change 'life-long' habits on a daily basis. Whether you are overcoming a phobia, a compulsion or any other neurological or physiological habit, the key is the same. If you weren't born with a cigarette in your mouth, you had to train and condition yourself to smoke – and if you learned it, you can unlearn it.

In the next session, we are going to take this process of quickly and easily changing habits and use it to completely change the habitual associations you make with smoking. As you will see, this will change a lot more than you think ...

•

Change Your Habits, Change Your Life

Change Your Habits, Change Your Life

In the course of putting together this book, I reviewed a number of the other stop-smoking systems currently on the market. One of the more interesting ones used what they called an 'extinction' programme (which I must admit I thought was a poor choice of words!).

The way the programme worked was that over the course of twelve weeks, you would gradually change the things you associated with smoking. In the first week you could smoke as many cigarettes as you wanted, just none after dinner. The next week was the same, but no cigarettes after dinner or in the first hour of the day. Each week you would eliminate one association until by the end of the twelve weeks, you had given up smoking altogether.

While I prefer to take care of things more quickly (if you haven't already, you can have completely quit smoking in the next few hours), the principle behind their system was sound. Human beings are creatures of habit and we associate things together. If you continually smoke cigarettes in your kitchen, after a time you will begin to associate being in your kitchen with wanting a cigarette.

In this system, we will be using the power of habitual association to help you to quit smoking today. I will be asking you to associate things you don't like with smoking, and to associate positive, empowering feelings with making positive choices and leading a healthier life.

Where do our associations come from?

Stop for a moment and imagine now the sound the cellophane wrapping makes as you open a new packet of your favourite brand of cigarettes. The cigarette slides smoothly out of the packet and you can taste the filter gently resting in your mouth. You hear the sound of the match striking the side of the box or the lighter firing up and can almost taste the sweet sensation of that first drag as it hits your mouth and the smoke is pulled down in to your lungs ...

Chances are that right now you are craving a cigarette a lot more than you were even a few moments ago. Yet all I did was make a few suggestions to your imagination and I was able to stimulate your desire for a cigarette.

Think about it this way:

If we can increase your desire for a cigarette in just a few moments, we can certainly decrease it over the course of this book.

Yet people are always telling me that they don't think they are suggestible – that they are above the influence of advertising. Sure they are. That's why cigarette companies spend millions of pounds on marketing every year, persuading and influencing you to smoke – because it doesn't work.

Look, face facts. You fell for it, and so did millions of other people. The evidence is right in front of you – you knowingly forced yourself to inhale poison on a daily basis.

The only reason people think that smoking makes them look cool or that a certain brand makes them look sophisticated is because advertising executives have been successful in installing that association in their heads.

Remember the Marlboro cowboy? His handsome face and rugged good looks helped to promote the idea that if you smoked Marlboro cigarettes, you too would be rough and strong. But nothing could be further from the truth.

Far from being a sign of strength, smoking is like a big neon sign of weakness. It says, 'I can't handle my emotions, so I have to use nicotine to help me. Cigarettes are in control of my life.'

In fact, two of the models who played the 'rough and ready' Marlboro cowboy, Wayne McLaren and David McLean, are sadly no longer with us. They both died slow and painful deaths from lung cancer.

Going unconscious

When we are addicted to something, we tend to have built up a significant positive association with it over time. Because of this, we don't make the effort to consider each time if we really want to do it or what it will cost us if we do – we just feel like we have to have it and we blindly follow that thought.

Think about it for yourself – the last time you lit up, did you stop and think: 'Do I really want *this* cigarette? Is now a good time to suck nicotine, tar and other cancer-causing agents into my body? How will I feel the next time I have to climb the stairs, or the next time I wake up in the morning? What kind of taste will I have in my mouth afterwards? How will I smell to the people around me whose opinion I really care about?'

My guess is, you barely even noticed the slight shift in the chemical balance in your body and the picture in your mind of you lighting up. You may not even have noticed the thought 'I'd like a cigarette' or even the mostly unconscious action of lighting up. That's because the entire process happens automatically in the space of under a second.

The brain is a mass of neural pathways and every action we take creates new connections. Every time we repeat an action, the neural pathway is strengthened, just like a footpath that becomes clearer and wider the more it is used. That is how a habit is formed.

For example, once upon a time, when you first tied your shoelaces, you really had to think about it, but now you can do it automatically. The repetition created a set of neural pathways, a programme in your unconscious mind. It's the same with smoking, you did it over and over until a habit was formed, a programme in the unconscious mind.

Everyone who tries to stop you from smoking tends to go on and on about the negative consequences of smoking in a crude attempt to change these associations. But you don't need to feel the pains in the chest before you stop smoking. You don't need to hear about cancer, gangrene or heart disease – you don't even need to read the 'smoking kills' labels on the side of a cigarette packet.

Cigarette companies love these warnings because they know that when most people who smoke stop to think about how dangerous it is, they have to have another cigarette to calm themselves down.

Instead of trying to 'scare you' into changing, we are going to rewrite the operating software of your mind. We are going to link some negative associations with smoking to help to destabilize this old compulsion. It's vitally important that we make the negative associations extremely strong in order to overcome the old positive association, so you may feel a little uncomfortable during this process. The good news is this – the more uncomfortable you feel, the better (and faster) the process is working.

In the last chapter, you created some positive associations with the thumb and middle finger of your **right** hand. In this next exercise, we are going to put negative feelings on your **left** hand. **Do not confuse the two.**

We will then begin to attach these negative feelings to cigarettes, which will begin to collapse the old, addictive positive ones and give your mind something to move away from. We will then transfer your positive feelings to the freedom of living without cigarettes, giving your mind something wonderful to move towards.

THE POWER OF ASSOCIATIONS

Before you do this technique for yourself, read through each step so that you know exactly what to do.

1 Think of a smell that you find totally disgusting. You need to be able to remember or imagine it vividly for this process to work well.

   For example, one of my clients imagined how Bernard Manning's underpants would smell after he'd been eating a vindaloo. Another one imagined inhaling the exhaust of a London bus. If either of those thoughts makes you feel disgusted, that's perfect!

2 Now imagine or remember that awful smell – what you notice as you breathe it in and how disgusted you feel. As you keep remembering this, squeeze your thumb and middle finger together on your **left hand**. Repeat this process as many times as you need until you feel utterly disgusted.

3 Next, think of a taste that you find utterly disgusting – it can be a food, beverage or anything at all. You need to find something that makes you feel really quite sick. (For example, how disgusted would you feel drinking the contents of a spittoon? What if it was filled with plenty of big green juicy lumps of phlegm?)

Remember, you need to find something that's totally repulsive in order for this process to work. Once again squeeze your left thumb and middle finger together and imagine swallowing that disgusting substance. Keep doing this over and over again, until you feel ready to retch!

4 Now, as you squeeze your left thumb and middle finger together, remembering how disgusting that smell and that taste are, imagine taking a little bit of a drag from a cigarette, then a bit more and more, gradually increasing the amount of cigarette smoke. Imagine that each time you inhale from a cigarette, a little bit more of that disgusting smell and taste is getting mixed in together with the smell and taste of the cigarette.

5 Keep repeating this process until you can no longer find anything but repulsion in the idea of smoking a cigarette.

If you have done this process correctly, you will now be feeling uncomfortable when you think about smoking. Great! That is evidence of how quickly the new programme can begin running inside your mind. As soon as you're ready, it's time to feel a lot better fast.

How good can it get?

Remember the 'calm' anchor you created in the previous session? We are now going to be associating even *more* good feelings with the thumb and middle finger on your right hand. (For the purposes of these exercises, it's very important that you do not confuse the two. Keep the repulsive feelings on your **left** hand and the positive ones on your **right** hand.)

We are going to programme your mind and body to release happy chemicals without cigarettes so that you automatically release good feelings at times when you used to smoke. This will not only reset your body's natural balance, it will also enable you to feel good whenever you want without the use of cigarettes, food or any other artificial stimulants.

We will do this by adding a stack of positive feelings to the 'calm anchor' you created in session two. So in a moment, we are going to remember some times in your life when you felt particularly good without cigarettes. Then we are going to create an association between those feelings and this squeeze of your fingers by repeating them together, over and over again.

Ready? Here we go ...

FROM CALM TO WONDERFUL, PART 1

Before you do this technique for yourself, read through each step so that you know exactly what to do.

1 Press the thumb and middle finger of your **right hand** together to fire off the 'calm anchor' you created in session two.

2 Now, remember a time you felt really, really good – you were having fun with friends, someone paid you a compliment, you felt incredibly loved. Return to it as though you were back there now. Remember that time vividly – see what you saw, hear what you heard and feel how good you felt.

3 As you keep going through that memory again and again, continue to squeeze your thumb and middle finger together on your right hand. Notice all the details, and make the images bigger and the colours richer, bolder and brighter. Make the sounds louder and crisper and the feelings stronger.

4 Next, think of a time that you felt DEEP PLEASURE. It needs to be intense and strong. As you keep going through that memory again and again, squeeze your thumb and middle finger together on your right hand. Recall it as vividly as possible. Remember that time, see what you saw, hear what you heard and feel how good you felt.

5 OK, stop and relax. You'll know that you've done this correctly when you squeeze your thumb and finger together and you feel that good feeling again. Go ahead do that now – just squeeze thumb and finger together and enjoy feeling these wonderful feelings.

Now we're going to programme good feelings to happen automatically whenever you are in a situation where you used to smoke. This will stop you from getting cravings and increase your overall sense of wellbeing ...

FROM CALM TO WONDERFUL, PART 2

1 Squeeze the thumb and middle finger of your right hand together again to get that good feeling going in your body.

2 Now imagine taking that good feeling with you into all the regular situations where you used to smoke, only this time imagine being there, feeling great without a cigarette. See what you'll see and hear what you'll hear as you take that good feeling into each one of those situations without any need for a cigarette.

3 Take yourself through a few difficult situations and handle each one of them perfectly. Here are a few examples:

• You're at work and it's a little stressful, but you are able to deal with it easily.

• You've had a drink or two and someone blows smoke in your direction. As they offer you a cigarette, you confidently say, 'No thanks – I don't smoke.' As you say those words, you realize they are true and feel even better.

• You've just finished an excellent meal. As you sit back and smile a contented smile, you think to yourself: 'You know what would make this perfect?' To your surprise, the words 'taking a deep breath and letting the good feelings intensify' come to mind. You smile even more deeply as you realize you can feel wonderful without a cigarette, enjoying a sense of natural comfort and satisfaction.

Imagine each scenario again and again until you feel really good about life without cigarettes but with more good feelings than ever before.

FREQUENTLY ASKED QUESTIONS ABOUT 'CHANGE YOUR HABITS, CHANGE YOUR LIFE':

Q. I've heard that you can smoke as much as you want as long as you stop by the time you're thirty. Why would I quit now?

Unfortunately, it's not as simple as that. Everyone is genetically different and there's no way of knowing how many cigarettes you can smoke before they kill you.

The human body is constantly rebuilding itself. Our body is made up of cells that are continually dividing and multiplying. For example, the liver, lungs and heart you have now are not the ones you had a few months ago. The speed at which these cells divide and multiply is carefully regulated. There are chemicals that speed up cell division and chemicals that slow the process down, like the accelerator and brakes on a car.

Every time you smoke a cigarette, you are weakening the brakes and putting pressure on the accelerator of your cells. When the balance between these two is interfered with by the toxins in the cigarette, the imbalance leads to mutated cells that continue to divide and multiply, resulting in a growth or tumour. These cells then invade neighbouring organs, thus spreading the disease. This is how cancer happens.

It is because every human being is different that you can't possibly know how close to that you are. If you have been smoking for a while you are playing Russian roulette – the next cigarette you have might be the one that triggers the mutation and ultimately kills you!

Q. What about all the people who smoke who don't get cancer?

Cancer is only one of the dangers from smoking. Nicotine increases the concentration of fatty acid in smoker's blood, and fatty deposits can reduce or block the blood supply in other parts of the body, leading to problems ranging from impotence to strokes to chronic lung disease to brain damage. Smoking also triples your risk of dying from heart disease, one of the leading causes of death in the UK.

And even if you don't actually die from smoking, the chances of your quality of life being destroyed are very high. More people get Chronic Obstructive Pulmonary Disease (COPD) than lung cancer. Smoking so damages the lungs that this irreversible disorder occurs: where you can no longer breathe on your own and you have to be permanently attached to an oxygen cylinder.

Q. OK, OK, I get it. Smoking is bad for me. But what if I smoke menthols or low-tar cigarettes?

Menthol cigarettes are not safer than other brands and may even be more dangerous. Menthol cigarettes produce a cool sensation in the throat when smoke is inhaled. People who smoke menthol cigarettes can inhale deeper and hold the smoke inside longer than smokers of non-menthol cigarettes. And sadly a low-tar cigarette can be just as harmful as a high-tar cigarette because a person often takes deeper puffs, puffs more frequently or smokes them to a shorter butt length. Studies have not found that the risk of lung cancer, heart disease or stroke is any lower in smokers of 'light' or low-tar cigarettes.

Q. Should I just kill myself now and get it over with?

Of course not! Not only does your recovery start almost immediately after your last cigarette (see the FAQ from session two), you can begin to experience more health, energy, vitality and inner and outer beauty within moments.

We'll begin creating those experiences for you in the very next session ...

SESSION FOUR

•

A New
Healthy You

A New Healthy You

The way we see ourselves affects everything about us. If you see yourself as a kind person, you are more likely to behave kindly towards others. If you think of yourself as someone with no willpower, you are more likely to give up long before someone who sees themselves as the kind of person who can make it through any difficulty and come out smiling.

Stop for a moment now and think about yourself. What images do you see in your mind's eye? What do you say to yourself about who and what you 'really' are? Psychologists refer to this way that you think of yourself as your 'self-image'. Our self-image is stored in our imagination, and acts as a sort of a blueprint we can refer to in order to know how to behave in a variety of situations. Yet this image is not fixed. Throughout your life, you've changed aspects of your self-image many times without even thinking.

Up until now, you have been thinking of yourself as 'a smoker'. You have probably referred to yourself that way so many times that you don't even notice any more – it's become part of your current self-image.

However, the next two powerful visualization techniques are going to begin the process of changing the way you perceive yourself from now on. We are going to change your self-image from that of 'a smoker' to 'a healthy, happy person'. You will start to see yourself as someone who used to smoke, but doesn't do that any more.

Changing your image of 'you'

For years, you thought of yourself as a child; then, one day, you began thinking of yourself as an adult. If you think back to how you used to dress or have your hair when you were younger, you may remember that was once 'you', but it's just not who you are any more. You have moved on in so many ways.

The same thing happens as you shed the self-image of yourself as 'a smoker'. Where did this image come from? You weren't born with a cigarette in your mouth, were you? In the same way as you learned to smoke, you had to learn to see yourself as a smoker – and you are now going to let that old habit and identity go, and see yourself the way you would ideally like to be.

Now, in just a moment I am going to ask you to visualize yourself. Some people believe they can't do this easily. But science has shown that *everybody* (barring people with neurological damage) has the ability to visualize. To prove this to yourself, answer the following questions:

• What colour is your front door?

• Which side is the handle on?

In order to answer either of these questions, you had to go inside your imagination and make a picture. These pictures will usually not be 'photo quality' – and that's a good thing. You need to be able to see the difference between what's real and what's imaginary. But the moment you begin to become aware of how you 'see' yourself in your mind, you can change the way you see yourself for life.

THE PICTURE OF HEALTH

Before you do this technique, read through each step so that you know what to do.

1   Imagine yourself as you'd ideally look if you were as healthy, happy and successful as you can imagine.

2   What do your eyes look like? What expression do you have on your face? What are you wearing? What sort of a confident posture do you have?

3   Next, make the image life-size, or even larger than life. Take a few moments to enjoy looking at that future you – the you you are becoming.

4   Now, float into the future you. See through their eyes, hear through their ears and feel what it feels like to be glowing with health, happiness and success. Say to yourself in a confident voice, 'This is who I really am!'

You can repeat this exercise as often as you like. When you've got a real sense of what it would be like to be this new, healthier you, step out and put your 'picture of health' to one side.

The SWISH pattern

Most people are completely unaware of the role internal pictures play in making decisions about what to do and how to behave. For example, if someone asks you to a party, you will make a picture in your imagination of how that party will be. If your picture is of you looking sad, being ignored in a room full of unfriendly people, you will probably choose not to go. If your picture is of you looking great in a room filled with attractive people who are having a wonderful time, laughing and enjoying your company, you will probably feel a desire to go to the party.

The same thing is true whether you are choosing food from a menu in a restaurant, which outfit to wear to the party, or whether or not to have another cigarette.

First, you make a picture in your mind of each possibility, then you make a decision about what to do. Of course, this decision-making process happens so quickly that most of us are completely unaware that it's going on all day long.

Up to now, a large part of how you motivated yourself to keep smoking was through these images you were making in your imagination. You make an attractive picture of yourself lighting a cigarette and bringing it close to your mouth, and before you know it you have an 'automatic' desire to smoke.

In a moment, we are going to change that unconscious decision-making process for good.

In the future, every time you think about smoking, it will seem less and less important, and your health, happiness and wellbeing will become more and more important.

What we are about to do is an amazing technique developed by Dr Richard Bandler, one of the world's leading researchers into the practical power of the mind. Through the use of two separate images, we are going to train your brain to move away from the behaviour of smoking and move towards a healthy empowered self.

Here's how it works. First, you will create an image of your hand coming up to your face to place a cigarette in your mouth. Just before the cigarette reaches your mouth, we are going to interrupt that old pattern with a big, bold image of you at your best – the picture of health you created in the previous exercise. Each time you do this, I want you to smash the old picture of the cigarette with a big, bright, bold picture of yourself as you would ideally like to be.

To put it simply, we are teaching your brain a new pattern:

Not 'that' – THIS!

This will not only cause a 'short-circuit' in the old decision-making process that led you to smoke, it will also create a new 'neural pathway' towards health. Each time your brain goes down this new path, it will get easier and easier for you to make new and different choices in the future. Each time you run through this exercise, you are conditioning yourself to automatically think and act differently from before.

In fact, the more you have smoked up until now, the faster you can change ...

THE SMOKING 'SWISH'

Before you do this technique, read through each step so that you know exactly what to do.

1 Think of the very last thing you are aware of before a cigarette goes into your mouth for the first time. It can be the sight of your fingers coming up towards your face, cigarette in hand; the sight of the lit match burning orange and red as you bring it up towards your hand; even your hand reaching into the packet or rolling the tobacco from a pouch.

Make sure you are seeing the image through your own eyes, as you would in real life. When you've got it, put it to one side for the moment.

2 Now, bring back the 'picture of health' you created in the last exercise. Enjoy looking at it for a few moments on a giant screen – bold, beautiful and larger than life. Now, imagine shrinking it down and pushing it way off into the distance until you can barely make it out.

3 Once again, imagine the picture of what happens just before you begin smoking.

4 Now, close your eyes and imagine your picture of health coming straight at you, growing bigger and bolder as it approaches until you can see it smashing the old smoker picture into tiny pieces and filling the screen in front of you. Take a moment to enjoy the good feelings, then briefly open your eyes.

5 Close your eyes again and repeat steps 3 and 4 at least ten more times, as fast as you can.

There are three ways to test how well you have done at creating a new, positive association to a healthy new you...

a Imagine the picture of what happens just before you would have begun smoking. If you have successfully created the new pattern, the old picture will feel different to you. You may even have difficulty bringing that old cigarette picture to mind.

b Imagine actually smoking a cigarette. Again, you will know you have successfully done the technique because the image of the healthy new you will be more appealing than the idea of smoking.

c If both 'a' and 'b' have been successful, take out a cigarette and go to light it up. If you really don't want to, congratulations!

Of course, if at some point in the future a bit of the old urge returns, you will be able to simply 'swish' it away following the same steps you used in the exercise above.

FREQUENTLY ASKED QUESTIONS ABOUT 'A NEW HEALTHY YOU'

Q. Help – I'm having trouble seeing myself in my mind!

While it is not necessary to actually 'see' yourself in your mind's eye as clearly as you can see yourself in a mirror, one simple way to enhance your picture of health is to first stand in front of a mirror. Pick out one detail of yourself in the mirror (perhaps your nose), then close your eyes and imagine just your nose floating in space or on a screen in front of you.

Each time you repeat this process, you can add in another detail until you are easily able to see yourself as you would ideally like to be.

Q. I notice you don't talk about becoming a 'non-smoker'. Is there a reason for this?

As you may already know, your mind cannot process a negative suggestion. In other words, if I instruct you not to think of a blue elephant, the only way you can carry out my instructions is to first think of a blue elephant and then to do whatever you can to remove the thought from your mind.

As we have discussed throughout this chapter, the image of yourself you hold in your mind will have a significant influence on your behaviour. Well-meaning as they may be, programmes that encourage you to think about yourself as a 'non-smoker' might as well be telling you to think of yourself as a 'non-blue elephant' – your self-image will be of a blue elephant, even if that elephant has a big red 'x' through it.

When you stopped wearing nappies, you didn't become a 'non-nappy wearer' – you just grew up and began acting in ways that were appropriate for what you had learned and who you were becoming. In the same way, you are not a 'non-smoker' – you are simply a person who no longer smokes.

In the next session, I am going to reveal the most powerful process in this entire system – a process which will enable you to say 'screw it!' and make the decision to quit smoking for the last time …

SESSION FIVE

•

Never Again!

Never Again!

By now, you may already have noticed a loss of interest in smoking cigarettes. It may even feel easy and almost natural for you to say the phrase, 'No thanks – I don't smoke.'

Whether you have already quit or are simply moving in that direction, many people find the technique I will be sharing with you in this chapter is enough to push them 'over the threshold' – past the point where it is now easier to say 'no' than to smoke yet another cigarette.

Past the point of no return

Nearly everyone has had the experience of getting to a point where they have just had enough and they tell themselves, 'Never again!'

Some people do it in the face of massive adversity – leaving a bad job or a bad relationship even though they are terrified of what might happen; giving up drugs or alcohol even though it feels as though they won't be able to cope. It is almost like a switch flicks on inside you, and you just know that no matter what, you will never go back to that old, destructive behaviour. A friend of mine became an alcoholic and ended up living on the streets. What finally got him to the point of 'never again' were two dramatic experiences that happened in quick succession.

The first was when he woke up one morning in the street to the sight and smell of a dog urinating on him. Later that day, he went to the funeral of a friend. He was so drunk that he fell into the empty grave with everyone watching. At some level, he probably recognized that as a message from his unconscious mind, that 'this is where you are going to end up if you don't stop this destructive habit'.

Of course, sometimes a 'never again' moment can be more discreet. Before I became a hypnotist, I was a successful radio broadcaster. As my interest in hypnotism grew, I tried for a time to do both things simultaneously. Inevitably, there came a point where I realized that I could do both things with mediocre results or that I'd have to choose one and do it really well. This was a tough decision for me – although I no longer really enjoyed being a DJ, it was comfortable and familiar. Quitting that job to become a hypnotist felt like taking a giant leap into the unknown.

I went back and forth about the decision, first imagining what my life would be like if I stayed in my familiar, safe 'rut', then imagining all the positives and negatives of my new choice. Each time I ran through these choices, I could feel myself getting more and more excited about the possibilities my new way of living might bring me.

I finally said 'screw it' and went to see the programme controller and told him that regrettably I had to quit. He nearly fell off his chair. After all, nobody just quits a job at Radio 1, especially when they didn't know exactly what the future would hold.

But I quit anyway. I walked out of his office with a knot in my stomach, but feeling more in control of my life than ever before. A week later I was offered my first TV show, and my life has become better and better from that moment of decision.

Nearly everyone I have ever met has moments like this in their own life – times when they have said to themselves, 'Fuck it – I am just going to do this!' In fact, the billionaire business entrepreneur Richard Branson's motto is 'screw it, let's do it'. He credits this ability to find more reasons to do something than not to do it with much of his phenomenal success in business and in life.

Let's take a few moments now to anchor this feeling of unstoppable determination to your decision to quit smoking forever ...

SCREW IT!

1 Take a few moments now to remember a time when you thought to yourself, 'Screw it – I am just going to go for it!' It might have been about something big or small, but either way, you could feel that unstoppable determination propel you in a positive direction.

2 Go back to that time in your mind – see it through your eyes, hear it through your ears and feel that feeling spread through your entire body.

3 Now, think about your decision to quit smoking forever. Notice how powerful you feel having made this decision while feeling these feelings. Actually hear yourself say the words 'Screw it – let's do it!' in your mind.

Over the threshold

When I first began helping people to quit smoking, I was particularly interested in why it was that some people were continually trying to quit (and failing), while others didn't even seem to think about it at all – one day they just quit completely and never smoked again.

What was the difference that made the difference? It turned out that they had all experienced a series of moments of emotional intensity in a very short space of time.

After all, most smokers think 'I really ought to give up' from time to time. Often, it's just a thought without much emotional intensity behind it. Even when there is some emotional intensity, say in the wake of hearing about someone diagnosed with cancer or a sudden pain in the chest, it usually remains as an isolated incident and it can be months or even years until the next significant emotional event.

Here is the key:

If several negatively emotionally charged smoking-related incidents happen in quick succession, the brain goes through an experience of overwhelm and your biological survival mechanism kicks in.

It works something like this: you get a chest pain, a close friend is diagnosed with cancer, several of your friends quit and you feel the social pressure, your partner quits, you find yourself short of breath or you went on a smoking binge and wake up with your mouth tasting like an ashtray.

If these incidents had happened in isolation with plenty of recovery time in between, they would not necessarily be enough to get somebody to quit. But when all these things happen around the same time, the critical mass of emotional negativity towards smoking pushes your brain through a threshold. Your brain starts to worry, a massive negative feeling builds up in your body, your primal protection mechanism kicks in and you say to yourself, 'Never again!' A strong negative association begins to build up towards smoking and it tips them over the edge, like the last straw that breaks the camel's back.

The wonderful thing is that you don't have to wait until you are actually experiencing serious health problems in the future in order to change. By vividly remembering four of the negative incidents you have had in relation to smoking over and over again, you can create an artificial threshold experience that will be every bit as effective as the ones that can happen spontaneously.

The reason this works is because the mind cannot tell the difference between a real or a vividly imagined experience. If you close your eyes and remember something scary in great detail, your body will produce a fear response. Similarly, if you vividly remember all the times and reasons you have thought 'I am going to quit smoking' over and over again, you will build up a mass of negative feelings about smoking and the growing sense of repulsion pushes you over the edge from 'smoker' to 'someone who used to smoke'.

THE THRESHOLD TECHNIQUE

The power of this technique comes from both the intensity of your feelings and the speed at which you run it, so it is especially important to really take the time to read through it completely several times before you actually do it ...

1 Call to mind the three times when you most enjoy or feel the need to smoke. (For example, first thing in the morning, at work, after dinner, etc.) If you like, write them down so it will be easy to remember them later.

2 Next call to mind four negative experiences with smoking where you felt like you really wanted or even had to quit smoking. Maybe you had a health scare, or you just felt repulsed by smoking. Once again, make a list of them so you can easily call them to mind.

3 Now run through the first of those four negative memories in great detail. Do it as though you were back inside the experience, reliving the moment completely. See the things you saw, hear the things you heard and feel completely the negative feelings you felt all over again, as though you are actually there.

4 Repeat the process with each one of the memories. Go through each memory again and again, one after another. Each time you do this, make the images bigger, brighter and more colourful so they are becoming more and more intense. Go through them faster and faster, until the events begin overlapping and the worst parts are happening over and over again, one after another after another.

5 Only when you have generated an overwhelmingly strong negative feeling throughout your body, think about having to smoke a cigarette. Imagine somebody is trying to force you to smoke, even though you no longer want to.

6 Now, run through each of the three times where in the past you would have enjoyed smoking. Imagine somebody forcing you to smoke in each of these three situations until you want to scream, 'Screw it – never again!'

Many people need to do this technique only once to feel totally free of their attachments to cigarettes. But if you want to you can do it carefully and thoroughly as many times as you need to in order to reinforce the effect.

FREQUENTLY ASKED QUESTIONS ABOUT 'NEVER AGAIN!'

Q. Maybe I'm just wishy-washy, but I can't recall ever saying 'screw it' or 'never again'. Does that mean these techniques won't work for me?

If you've really never felt a strong desire to quit, why have you read this far into the book?

My advice is to go visit a cancer ward, or go on the internet and read about the exact details of what nicotine is doing to your body on a daily and even hourly basis. If you really can't generate these feelings, it's highly likely you will remain a smoker until the day you die. (And research shows that on average that day will come about fourteen years sooner that it needs to ...)

Q. I've run through the threshold technique several times and it just makes me feel bad. Do I really need to do this?

Again, yes. The idea isn't to make yourself feel bad; it's to make yourself feel bad enough to actually change. Think about it – if you feel repulsed by cigarettes, will you find it easier not to smoke them? Of course, once you've made the decision to quit, you can immediately begin to replace those feelings with the sense of calm and wellbeing you began cultivating in the second session.

In the next session, I will be sharing two powerful techniques that have been scientifically proven to change the chemistry of your body to reduce and even eliminate cravings. Having these techniques at your fingertips will allow you to stick to your decision without feeling undue stress and without gaining any weight at all ...

SESSION SIX

•

An End
to Cravings

An End to Cravings

Even after people have given up smoking, they often wonder how long it will last and what will happen if those cravings start to come back. Without the tools and knowledge you are learning in this book, you would do one of three things in response to these cravings:

1 **Smoke another cigarette.** After all, however bad it might be, at least you know it worked in the past.

2 **Eat fatty or sugary foods.** The simple sugars in these foods would give you a quick (if ultimately self-defeating) endorphin release and the craving would disappear.

3 **Nothing.**

The fact is that if you just stuck it out for a few days, those cravings would disappear all by themselves. Your body would quickly return to its own natural equilibrium and the endorphins would start to flow on their own once again without needing a cigarette to control them.

This is exactly what many people do, who 'just quit'. They tough it out for a few days until their body's natural chemical balance returns.

If you like, you can do the same thing. But why not make it easy on yourself?

In this session, I am going to show you exactly how to knock out any cravings in a matter of moments. And when you know that you can handle any cravings if and when they come up, you no longer need to smoke or eat in an attempt to control them.

The healing power of oxygen

When people smoke, more than half of what they breathe is fresh air – pulled through the cigarette right down into the lungs. People don't normally breathe as deeply as they do when they are smoking, so each deep breath actually changes how you feel by putting more oxygen into your bloodstream.

This means you can use deep breaths to change the way you feel instantly and begin to take control over cravings. Let's do this now ...

A BREATH OF FRESH AIR

1 Breathe all the way out as far as you can until there's no air left in your lungs.

2 When you can't breathe out any further, stop pushing and wait until your next in-breath happens automatically. Notice where in your body you can feel the fresh oxygen you are breathing go.

3 Breathe once or twice normally. When you are ready, once again breathe all of the air out of your body until your lungs are empty. Feel the sensations in your body until it naturally breathes in all by itself. Again, notice which parts of your body are being most nourished by the fresh oxygen you are breathing in.

4 After a few more normal breaths, once again exhale all the air from your lungs. Enjoy the feelings of relaxation and tingling you are feeling in your body, and when the in-breath comes, notice where the oxygen goes.

5 Allow your breathing to normalize and return to your day, feeling refreshed.

Whenever you experience a craving for a cigarette in the future, you can use this technique – breathe all the way out, let go and feel your body breath fresh oxygen in. Do it three times in a row and you will be amazed at how different you are feeling. In fact, most people find any cravings have disappeared before they even get to the third breath.

While this simple technique is deceptively powerful, there is another way of defeating cravings that not only eliminates them in the moment but has been proven to actually change the structure of your brain in a way that can eliminate them from ever occurring again.

The real cause of addiction

In 1981, a scientist named Bruce Alexander began an extraordinary experiment to test the causes of addiction in society. While most scientists at the time felt that addiction was a primarily bio-chemical event, Alexander was intrigued by the possibility of environmental causes for addiction, based on the fact that of the thousands of soldiers who regularly used heroin during the Vietnam War, an extraordinary 90 per cent of them quit on returning home with minimal withdrawal symptoms or cravings.

What Alexander did was take caged rats in a lab and get them heavily addicted to morphine over a period of months by mixing the drug with sugar in their water supply. He then divided the rats into two groups. One group remained in their cages; the others were placed into a sort of a 'garden of Eden' for lab rats which he and his colleagues lovingly dubbed 'Rat Park'.

Rat Park had wide open spaces, readily available food and drink, and warm comfortable housing. It was filled with grass, trees and even toys for the rats to play with.

Having divided the rats between cages and Rat Park, he presented each group of 'addicted' rats with the choice of fresh, unsweetened water or the morphine-laden sugar water. It was at this point something absolutely amazing happened – *without exception*, the rats in the cages chose to remain addicted while the Rat Park rats immediately switched over to the regular water, despite going through withdrawal symptoms from the morphine over a period of several days. This in spite of the fact that the rats had all been addicted to the morphine for a significant period before giving it up in a single day.

What conclusion can we draw from this experiment?

According to the brilliant researcher Dr Ronald Ruden, author of *The Craving Brain*, studies into the source of cravings for cigarettes, food, sex, alcohol or drugs of any sort indicates that not only is your environment a significant factor in addiction but that your *internal* environment (what he calls 'the landscape of your brain') may be far *more* significant than your external environment.

Ruden has shown that the key factor in creating an internal environment conducive to addictive behaviour is the presence of 'inescapable stress' – an ongoing sense that nothing can be done to reduce the amount of stress you are experiencing in your life.

That seemingly inescapable stress may take the form of homelessness, poverty, a bad marriage or a chronic illness or even something as simple as stress at work. It can even be caused by guilt or shame – the regret for something which happened in the past that 'can never be undone'.

Even people from very wealthy families, who from the outside seem to have everything, can suffer from this kind of stress and end up as addicts. Their inescapable stress may come from a fear of not being good enough, a sense of being unloved, or simply being unable to live up to everyone's expectations of who and what they were supposed to be.

Based on Dr Alexander and Dr Ruden's research, we now have a 'magic pill' to help you quit smoking:

**You've been stressed (for whatever reason),
so you've been smoking.**

**Control your response to stress
and you will no longer want or need to smoke.**

Biologically speaking, if every time you would have smoked in the past you now eat, run, meditate or 'tough it out', you would still be considered to be addicted. Although you have substituted a healthier activity for the old, unhealthy response, you would still be dealing with cravings. Even under these circumstances you can quit for life – it's just that there will always be an element of struggle.

What most people do when they first quit smoking is turn to food as a way of dealing with their stress, which is the main reason so many people who quit temporarily gain weight and then go back to smoking again. As long as they continue eating in response to their stress, they don't need to smoke – but as the pounds pile on and they decide they need to control their eating, the urge to smoke returns as strong as ever.

But that does NOT mean that the best we can hope for is to replace our unhealthy addictions with healthy ones. As you reprogramme your mind and develop your ability to respond to stress without the crutch of cigarettes, you will change the neuro-chemical landscape of your brain. Cravings begin to disappear completely, and smoking, overeating or any other excessive or drug-based response to stress will be as unappealing to you as the morphine-laced sugar water was to the residents of Rat Park.

Changing the landscape of your brain

Thought Field Therapy, or TFT, is an extraordinary set of techniques created by Dr Roger Callaghan and has been the subject of numerous medical studies into its effectiveness as a short- and longer-term cure for a wide variety of problems. It has been repeatedly proven to increase your body's production of 'happy chemicals' such as serotonin, and reduce 'stress chemicals' such as adrenaline and noradrenalin. This not only makes the physical cravings go away in the moment, over time it actually changes the internal landscape of your brain.

After using the technique I am about to share with you a number of times, your brain will no longer be able to produce the old craving response to external or internal stress. Any time you do have a craving, it's another opportunity to reprogramme your brain. Soon, you will have overwritten the operating software of your brain and the cravings will disappear for good.

The effect of tapping in the specific sequence I will share with you is to reset the way that your brain interprets and responds to stress, thereby altering your internal brain structure. We will be concentrating upon any feelings of craving or intense, nagging desire for a cigarette.

You will need to be able to really concentrate for a few minutes, as it is important that you continue focusing on the craving feeling as you follow my instructions.

These instructions entail tapping on specific acupuncture

meridian points in the order and sequence I describe. It does not matter whether you use your right or left hand or whether you tap on the right or left side of the body. Both sides have the same effect, so simply use whichever side and whichever hand comes naturally.

THE TAPPING TECHNIQUE

Before you do this technique, read through each step so that you know exactly what to do.

1 I want you get the biggest desire for a cigarette that you can, right now. If you don't have a big enough craving, put this technique to one side and come back to it when you are really feeling it.

2 Focus on this craving for a moment, and when you've thought of that I'd like you to rate your desire for a cigarette on a scale of 1 to 10, with 1 being the lowest and 10 the highest. This is important, because in a moment we want to know how much you've reduced it.

3 On a scale of 1 to 10, how strong is your craving? Remember, if you're not gagging for a smoke (i.e. your craving is not at least a 7), come back to this technique later.

4 Now take two fingers of either hand and tap about ten times under your collarbone while you continue to think about having a smoke.

5 Now tap under your eye ten times.

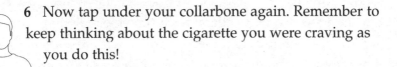

6 Now tap under your collarbone again. Remember to keep thinking about the cigarette you were craving as you do this!

7 Place your other hand in front of you and tap on the back of it between your ring finger and your little finger. Continue to think about smoking a cigarette as you do this and each of the steps that follow:

- Close your eyes and open them.
- Keep your head still, keep tapping and look down to the right, then down to the left.
- Keep tapping and rotate your eyes round 360 degrees clockwise, and now 360 degrees anti-clockwise.

Remember to keep thinking about the cigarette you were craving as you do this!

- Now hum the first few lines of 'Happy Birthday' out loud.
- Count out loud from 1 to 5.
- Once again hum the first lines of 'Happy Birthday' out loud.

8 Stop and check – on a scale from 1 to 10, what number is your craving at now?

If it hasn't completely gone yet, just repeat this sequence again until it does.

If the craving returns at some point in the future, just run through this sequence again. Each time the craving returns it will be less intense than the last and it will take less time to knock out. Soon you will be able to knock out any craving in a matter of seconds, and in time the cravings will disappear altogether.

(If you are having a craving for food instead of cigarettes, please read the bonus session on 'The Simplest Weight-Loss System in the World'.)

FREQUENTLY ASKED QUESTIONS ABOUT 'AN END TO CRAVINGS'

Q. I love the tools you are giving me to handle the mental aspect of smoking, but are there any things that will help with the physical side?

The first thing to remember is that the desire to smoke cigarettes is more mental than physical. While using the tapping technique will change the physical landscape of your brain, the actual physical addiction to nicotine will be completely gone within a few weeks.

Any urge to smoke you may experience after that time will be psychological, not physical. In other words, even though you may experience it in your body, you create it in your mind. As you practise the techniques in this book and listen each day to the accompanying CD, you will be reprogramming your mind to get rid of those cravings forever.

The second thing to remember is that when you were smoking, you were in the habit of attempting to control your stress and boredom with cigarettes. So any time you may have tried to quit in the past, you began to feel more stress and boredom. The endorphins in your body were sitting there waiting for the next signal from a cigarette to release into your bloodstream and make you feel good. By practising the techniques in this system, you are resetting your body's endorphin-release mechanism so you can easily feel good without a cigarette at times you used to smoke.

Here are some additional tips:

- Many smokers use cigarettes to give themselves little breaks during the day. Taking a break is good for you, so carry on taking that time off – but do something different. Walk round the block, have a cup of tea or drink of water, or do some of the techniques on this programme.

- If possible, drink a lot of fruit juice. When you stop smoking, the body goes through a big change. The blood sugar levels tend to fall, the digestion is slowed down and your body starts to eject the tar and poisons that have accumulated. Fresh fruit juice contains fructose, which restores your blood sugar levels, vitamin C which helps clear out impurities, and high levels of water and fibre to keep your digestion going. Alternatively, eat at least one piece of fruit every day for the first two weeks after you have stopped.

- Notice if you can cut your caffeine intake by about half. Nicotine breaks down caffeine in the bloodstream, so without the nicotine a little bit of coffee will have a big effect.

Q. Why won't I gain weight? Nearly everyone I know gained weight when they tried to give up smoking!

You won't gain weight because, unlike in other systems, we are dealing with the cause (your stress response), not the symptom (smoking). Old-fashioned hypnotists would merely give their clients suggestions like 'you no longer smoke', 'the idea of smoking makes you nauseous', 'you are disgusted by the smell and taste of cigarettes', etc.

While this would often be enough to get people to stop smoking (we used some similar techniques in session three), it didn't address the real cause of smoking – the sense of inescapable stress going on inside and around you. Because I am giving you tools to deal with the stress as well as the cigarettes, you will be able to completely give up cigarettes without having to stick food or anything else in your mouth as a way to change your feelings.

In addition, each time you use the CD, you will be both reducing your stress in the moment and reprogramming your mind to experience a greater sense of wellbeing in the future. That's why it's so important that you **listen to the CD every day for at least two weeks**. The more you listen, the easier your transition from smoking to healthy living will be.

In the next session, we will complete our time together in this book with two exercises that will change the way you think about the future and make it easy to decide once and for all how you most want to live in the world …

•

Creating a
Positive Future

Creating a Positive Future

Having worked with people from every walk of life over the past twenty years, I have come to realize that one of the main differences between the people who succeed and the ones who don't is their ability to think about the long-term consequences of each and every decision they make.

Focusing on the possibility of a wonderful romantic relationship makes asking someone out on a date easier to do, even if it can seem a bit difficult or scary while you're doing it.

Similarly, far fewer people would choose the fleeting pleasure of an affair if in the moment of choice, they were able to stop and think intensely about the downside – a heartbroken spouse, devastated children and the financial cost of divorce.

And smoking in many ways is worse. Not only can you lose everything you hold dear to you, you lose your health as well – and the momentary pleasure of a cigarette is rarely equal to the pain that ultimately awaits the person who smokes it.

Yet I am amazed at the number of people I meet every year who have never really thought about the consequences of their actions on their long-term future. They spend hours each day thinking about what they want to have for dinner, watch on TV or do over the weekend, but next to no time at all thinking about what they would really love to have happen to them in their lives.

One of the reasons for this is that human beings tend to engage in repetitive behaviours (like smoking) which help maintain the sense of continuity between yesterday and today. Studies have shown that people crave this sense of familiarity and will tend to filter out anything that doesn't fit with their idea that 'tomorrow will be pretty much the same as today'.

But even if things are absolutely amazing and exactly the way you want them to be, the nature of life is change. So if you want next year to be better than this one, you need to begin planning for better things to happen.

A new perspective on the future

I mentioned my uncle John earlier in this book. But I didn't say what happened to my father. Although he was born nearly ten years earlier than my uncle John, he is still alive today, healthy and happy. My father used to smoke too, just like my uncle John. The only difference was, my father made the decision to quit.

Now I'm sure that if Uncle John could have seen that he was going to die such a dreadful death so young, leaving his grieving family sobbing by his bedside, he would have stopped smoking no matter what it took. But hindsight is like that – it's easy to look back and see what we should have decided a long time ago.

That's why we are now going to get you some hindsight ahead of time. We are going to have a good look at where you will end up if you stay smoking and where you will end up when you quit. This will help you to view each cigarette and the whole idea of smoking in a more realistic, long-term perspective.

Many smokers I have worked with over the years think only about the next cigarette they are going to have and the pleasure or relief from stress they think it will give them. They don't seem to have any representation of what future that cigarette is creating for them. In fact, some of them don't want to even look.

Although they hope it won't happen, many of the smokers I have met actually expect to die early from a horrible death.

The danger of this kind of subconscious expectation is that it can end up becoming a self-fulfilling prophecy. As my uncle John might have said with the benefit of hindsight:

**You are not a god – you are not the exception.
It can happen to you.**

In order to change, we need to look intensely into the horrible future that awaits you unless you make a strong commitment to yourself today. But at the same time, we will look into the positive future you can begin creating now. You will see some of the many wonderful effects of quitting smoking – longer life, better health, more energy, and staying younger for longer.

Rather than focus on what you would be 'missing out on' in the moment, you will create a new perspective that reveals both the long-term costs of smoking and the long-term benefits of quitting. This is why in order to get maximum effect from it, you will need to be prepared to use your imagination as vividly as possible ...

A SIMPLE DECISION

Before you do this technique, read through each step so that you know exactly what to do.

1 I want you to imagine that you continue to smoke until the end of your life. In your mind now, travel out into the future to a point near the end of your life.

2 Notice what your health is like and the quality of your life. Ask yourself: What regrets do I have? What do I wish I'd done differently?

3 Return back to the present moment with your insights.

4 Now, imagine that you quit smoking today, and in your imagination I want you to once again travel out into the future to a point near the end of your life.

5 Notice what your health is like and the quality of your life. Ask yourself: What am I most grateful for in my life? What am I glad I did when I was younger?

6 Return back to the present moment with your insights.

7 Now, compare the two futures. What will your long-term future be like if you continue smoking? What will it be like if you quit?

8 Compare and contrast these two possible futures at least ten times, until it is a simple decision what future you want to create and what choice you will be making in the present to create it now.

You become what you think about

Through the course of this book, you have learned to reduce your stress levels by using a positive anchor. You have changed your associations to smoking (remember Bernard Manning's underpants?), and swished your self-image from that of 'a smoker' to that of a healthy person who used to smoke. You have taken yourself to a place of 'never again', and learned that you can easily overwhelm any craving for a cigarette by taking three deep breaths or tapping it away for good.

Even though you may have already noticed the many changes you have been making, we are now going to programme your mind to make this new way of being an automatic part of your future.

For anything to happen in the real physical world, it first has to happen in the human imagination. That's why when I help someone to quit smoking forever, I teach them to practise thinking about a healthy, happy future again and again until they can see it in their mind's eye.

We are now going to train your mind in the same way to automatically move towards a more and more positive image of yourself. You are going to programme yourself to automatically see yourself in the future as healthy, happy and vibrantly alive ...

BETTER AND BETTER AND BETTER

Before you do this technique, read through each step so that you know exactly what to do.

1 Squeeze your thumb and finger together on your **right hand** and remember the really good feelings you have created inside you.

2 Now imagine waking up **tomorrow** *feeling even better* without smoking. See yourself living the major moments of tomorrow without any desire for cigarettes, proud of having changed your old habits and leaving your old addiction behind. Imagine how happy you are with your new healthy lifestyle.

3 Now imagine waking up **next week** *feeling even better* without smoking. See yourself living the major moments of your life without any desire for cigarettes, proud of having changed your old habits and leaving your old addiction behind. Imagine how happy you are with your new healthy lifestyle.

4 Now imagine waking up **next month** *feeling even better*. See yourself living the major moments of your life without any desire for cigarettes, proud of having changed your old habits and leaving your old addiction behind. Imagine how happy you are with your new healthy lifestyle.

5 Now imagine waking up **six months** from now, *feeling even better*. See yourself living the major moments of your life, proud of having changed your old habits and leaving your old addiction behind. Imagine how happy you are with your new healthy lifestyle.

6 Now imagine waking up **a year** in the future, *feeling even better*. See yourself living the major moments of your life, and imagine how happy you are with your healthy lifestyle. If you like, you can look back on that time you used to smoke as a dim and distant memory ...

FREQUENTLY ASKED QUESTIONS ABOUT 'CREATING A POSITIVE FUTURE'

Q. What's wrong with me? I have done everything and it still hasn't worked!

I'm sorry, but you haven't done everything. Have you gone through and done each and every exercise, imagining things in vivid detail? Have you listened to the CD every day for at least two weeks? Have you used the tapping protocol any time you felt a craving over the first few weeks after quitting? Have you given up your story about why YOU are the exception to the rule?

Most importantly of all, have you really *decided* to quit?

If you have, your success is inevitable and things will get easier and easier for you. If not, it's not too late to go back and do it again now.

Q. I've definitely made the decision to quit for good, but am worried that one day I may slip up and smoke a cigarette. Does that mean I have to do the whole system again?

Many people think that if they have one cigarette, they have once again 'become a smoker'. But remember, you never were a smoker – just someone who used to smoke and no longer does.

Congratulate yourself on having quit for as long as you have, pick yourself up, dust yourself off, and revisit any of the lessons that seem important to you. Listen to the CD some more. Remind yourself of your reasons for deciding to quit and recondition your mind for success.

Remember, in the end it comes down to a simple question of who's in charge – you or the cigarettes?

SOME FINAL THOUGHTS ON
Quit Smoking Today
Without Gaining Weight

Congratulations!

By reading this book all the way through to the end, you have demonstrated your commitment and ability to quit smoking not only today, but for the rest of your healthier, happier life.

Here are a few things that will help reinforce the changes you have already made on the inside:

1 If you haven't already done each of the exercises in the book, go back and do them now. While I have designed them so that you will receive the maximum benefit from doing them in the order they appear in the book, if there is a particular exercise that appeals to you, you may begin with that one first.

2 If you have done the exercises, make a note of the ones that seemed particularly impactful so that you can easily return to them over the next few days, weeks and months, whenever you desire. Remember, each exercise will take you only a few minutes to do, so you can do them as often as you like.

3 Listen to the CD. Listen to the CD, listen to the CD, listen to the CD. I cannot emphasize strongly enough the incredible changes that will take place through the regular listening to this hypnotic recording. Whether you have already quit or are just wondering if you have, listening to the CD will help ease your transition from smoker to 'someone who used to smoke'.

And that's it!

I've included a 'short form' of my weight-loss system in the appendix in case you're still concerned about maintaining a healthy weight. As for your appearance, now that you have stopped filling your body with toxins, you will become more and more attractive as your body replaces each of the old, toxic cells with new, healthy, vital ones.

May you live fully all your days, and may each day bring you closer to having all the things you most want in your life.

To your good health!

Paul McKenna

The Simplest Weight-Loss System in the World

The Simplest Weight-Loss System in the World

My weight-loss system has been proven the most effective in the world. One reason it works so well is that it's so simple – four golden rules to follow each time you eat. The other is because it's based on what actually works for naturally thin people around the world.

What follow are just the very basics you need not only to maintain your current weight but to begin to shed pounds if you are not yet at your optimal weight for health and wellbeing.

If you want to learn more, please refer to *I Can Make You Thin*, available from your local bookseller or from www.paulmckenna.com.

GOLDEN RULE NUMBER ONE:
WHEN YOU ARE HUNGRY, EAT

Why would anyone eat if they weren't hungry?

Well, you may have already guessed that one of the main reasons people eat when they do is simply habit. Like the faulty programming that caused you to smoke, the habit of eating only at prescribed times throughout the day is one of the main culprits in ignoring and overriding your body's innate wisdom.

Many people are so desensitized to their body's messages that they've forgotten how to pay attention. If you read Golden Rule above and said to yourself, 'But I'm hungry all the time!' or 'But I'm never hungry!', then this may be what has happened to you. Fortunately, as soon as you begin to make friends with your body again, you will once again be able to recognize the subtle and not so subtle signs of authentic hunger.

Here's the good news:

**All you need to do to reset your body's innate wisdom
is to eat whenever you feel hungry.**

Within a few days, your metabolism will stabilize and your body will relax, taking only those nutrients it truly needs to meet the requirements of the moment and easily eliminating the rest.

GOLDEN RULE NUMBER TWO:
EAT WHAT YOU WANT, NOT WHAT YOU THINK YOU SHOULD

As soon as you tell yourself not to eat certain foods (usually because you've been told they're bad for you), you upset the natural balance of your relationship with them. Rather than wanting it less, that 'forbidden food' instantly becomes more attractive to you. The inner battle between your positive intention and your resistance to being controlled (even by yourself) can be exhausting. As you begin to make peace with food and learn to listen to the wisdom of your body, you experience freedom from the tension and guilt that comes from not following your intuition.

Also, as you stop resisting and start to follow your natural intuitions about what to eat when, you may notice your tastes changing. You may even find yourself naturally attracted to the very foods you're 'supposed' to be eating now.

GOLDEN RULE NUMBER THREE:
EAT CONSCIOUSLY AND ENJOY EVERY MOUTHFUL

People who are overweight often shovel food into their mouths as quickly as possible in order to get a serotonin high. Unfortunately, because they are eating unconsciously, they never notice the signal from their stomach that lets them know they are full. So they keep on stuffing their faces, expanding their stomachs and putting on weight.

The problem is that even though they feel temporarily high from cramming in lots of food, they feel fat and guilty afterwards. In fact, they feel so bad that they repeat the whole ritual of unconsciously stuffing themselves again in order to anaesthetize the bad feelings they just created!

Here is perhaps the single most important key to success with my system:

You can eat whatever you want, whenever you want, so long as you fully enjoy every single mouthful.

I cannot emphasize this enough. I mean really enjoy it – savour the taste, and enjoy the wonderful textures and sensations as you thoroughly chew each mouthful.

If all you did for the next two weeks was to slow your eating speed down to about a quarter of what it used to be and chew each mouthful thoroughly, you will find any excess weight begins to fall away before you know it.

GOLDEN RULE NUMBER FOUR:
WHEN YOU THINK YOU ARE FULL, *STOP* EATING

The natural design of the human body is to eat when we're hungry and stop when we're satisfied, but many of us are conditioned to eat until we think we're full – or even worse, until whatever food we put on our plate is gone.

To lose weight effortlessly and keep it off, you must begin working with your body and not against it. To get slim and stay slim we need to resensitize ourselves to our 'inner thermostat' so we can stop eating when we are full and feel good for the rest of the day. In reality, when you've eaten enough, your stomach sends a signal: a sensation that says, 'I'm satisfied – that's enough.' Most people experience this gentle, clear, satisfied sensation in their solar plexus (the area below your ribcage but above your stomach).

Of course, if you miss this warm feeling of satisfaction when it first occurs, you'll notice that each subsequent bite of food becomes a little less enjoyable than the one before. The more you pay attention to it, the more obvious it becomes.

The Hunger Scale

Take a few moments right now to look at the hunger scale and tune into your body. How hungry are you right now?

Each person is different, but as a general rule, you want to eat whenever you notice yourself between 3 and 4 on the scale – that is when you are fairly hungry, but before you become ravenous. If you wait until you get down to 1 or 2, your body will go into starvation mode and you'll wind up probably eating more than your body needs and storing the excess as fat.

The Hunger Scale

1 – Physically faint
2 – Ravenous
3 – Fairly hungry
4 – Slightly hungry
5 – Neutral
6 – Pleasantly satisfied
7 – Full
8 – Stuffed
9 – Bloated
10 – Nauseous

Ideally, you'll want to stop eating at right around 6 or 7 on the hunger scale – when you are feeling pleasantly satisfied or full but not yet stuffed or bloated.

Of course, if you have been a serial dieter you may be so used to overriding your body's signals that you may at times 'forget to eat' until you're ravenous, or keep eating until you're full or even stuffed before noticing it's time to stop. If you think this might be you, practise tuning into your body once an hour until you begin to notice differences between different points on the scale.

The more you practise tuning into your own hunger, the sooner you'll be able to recognize your body's subtle signals, long before your stomach growls and your brain starts to get fuzzy.

Can it really be this simple?

Yes! Let's review the four elements of the system:

1 Eat whenever you are hungry.

2 Eat only what you want, never what you think you 'should'.

3 Eat consciously and enjoy every mouthful.

4 Stop when you even think your body is full.

That is all you need to do in order to lose weight and keep it off for life!

Index of techniques

To train personally with Paul McKenna
call 0845 230 2022

www.paulmckenna.com